AURAS

An Essay On The MEANING OF COLORS

By

Edgar Cayce

A.R.E. Press • Virginia Beach • Virginia

ISBN 87604-012-1

47th Printing, November 2006

Printed in Canada

PREFACE

THE essay herein contained is the last labor to which Edgar Cayce put his hand. The color chart was returned to me with corrections in his own hand awkwardly written. With it was a note, also written in longhand. "I cannot use my typewriter," it said. "I have lost the use of my left arm and my right leg is numb. I presume I have had a slight stroke."

That was in September. A month before, on my porch here in Clearwater, while we watched the porpoises sporting in the Gulf of Mexico and admired the spectacular sunsets, the booklet was planned. The human aura was one of our favorite subjects of conversation; whenever we got together I questioned him about his ability to see colors emanating from persons, and he always had some new and interesting anecdotes concerning this strange power, which because it functioned while he was fully conscious, in many, many ways intrigued him more than his gift for giving readings. At least it entertained him more at the moment it was taking place, for despite all the readings he gave, he never heard one. During all of the most interesting portions of his life he was asleep.

We were in the process of working out a new publication program during this visit, and it occurred to me that a short but instructive article on auras would be helpful to members of the Association, particularly if it carried Mr. Cayce's interpretation of the colors, worked out over a long period of years by patient trial and error. I made the suggestion to him, and he gave me the usual answer—that he didn't know enough about the subject, had no background in it, etc., ad infinitum. He had a very low opinion of anything he said while awake. I then put it differently. I asked him if he would collaborate with me, and since he apparently had not the power to refuse me anything I asked (any more than he had the power to refuse anyone else) he said yes.

We set to work immediately, right there on the porch, and I began making notes. By the time the text was ready he had returned to Virginia Beach, had fallen ill, and was at Roanoke resting. Early in December he was brought home to the house on Arctic Crescent. There, on the night of January 3, 1945, he passed away.

I remember him from those August days for so many things. He was so thin and tired and wistful. Yet his face lighted with transcendent joy when he saw me enter the water and slosh away on my own, swimming on my back in the warm, still water. He loved the Australian pines in front of our cottage, and wanted to have some sent to Virginia Beach, to plant along the lake behind the house. He was disappointed when he learned that they would not flourish that far north.

"Then I will have to come down here," he said. "You find a place, and we will get it together. I can rest here. I dreamed the other night that I was on a train coming to Florida. I had retired, and was going to live here."

I urged him to remain longer with me; I pressed him to give up the interminable, punishing hours he put in at the mounting stacks of correspondence. I suggested that he spend his time fishing and gardening, except for the periods when the readings were given. But these requests were to him unreasonable. In the letters which came to him were tales of misfortune and suffering. Each was a cry for help. He would have heard it as well in the garden or on the dock. If he could have answered it at once he would not have minded so much. But when he had to put off the reading —at first for weeks, then for months, then for a year or more, his heart was heavy and his mind became numb with the burden of his helplessness. Though he stayed asleep longer than ever before and pushed his output of readings to unprecedented heights, he could make but a small dent in the pile of requests. It was this more than anything which broke him.

On the day he left we drove with him as far as Lakeland. Along the way we stopped and ate a picnic lunch. Together we rehearsed our plans: publication and research were gradually to work their way to the fore of the Association's work, giving to everyone the wisdom and instruction of the readings.

Gradually he was to slacken his own work until it was devoted mainly to general readings on research subjects and for guidance and instruction. In this way the best that he had to give would be available to all. That way he would live long and help everyone, we were sure.

At Lakeland he stepped from the car and turned to smile at me and squeeze my hand. "Well, when we meet again we'll have everything worked out fine," he said. October was the date we had set. He would return then for a longer rest.

But the dreams that came to him here in our sunshine, and the whispers he heard in the Australian pines, were promises from another land. He will rest there, and just as he said, when we meet again we'll have everything worked out fine.

Two days after his death the proofs of this booklet arrived. In them is his final message, a plea for faith, hope, and charity, and above all, the courage and wisdom to engage in what Stephen MacKenna described as, "an active mental life, with a little love to warm it." For the burden of all the readings is the necessity for man to take up his cross—"Mind is the builder: knowledge not lived becomes sin; in every person of whatever station look not for things to criticize, but for something you adore in your Creator; for you will not enter the kingdom of heaven, except leaning upon the arm of someone you have helped."

—**Thomas Sugrue**

Clearwater Beach, Fla.,

January 15, 1945.

NOTE: Thomas Sugrue, author of *There is a River,* the authoritative biography of Edgar Cayce, was the victim of a rare paralytic disease, and was saved from complete immobility and almost certain death by Mr. Cayce's "readings" for him. This preface, written a few days after Edgar Cayce's death, reveals the deep personal and spiritual bond between the two men.

AURAS

EVER SINCE I can remember I have seen colors in connection with people. I do not remember a time when the human beings I encountered did not register on my retina with blues and greens and reds gently pouring from their heads and shoulders. It was a long time before I realized that other people did not see these colors; it was a long time before I heard the word aura, and learned to apply it to this phenomenon which to me was commonplace. I do not ever think of people except in connection with their auras; I see them change in my friends and loved ones as time goes by—sickness, dejection, love, fulfillment—these are all reflected in the aura, and for me the aura is the weathervane of the soul. It shows which way the winds of destiny are blowing.

Many people are able to see auras; many have had experiences similar to mine—not knowing for many years that it was something unique. One of my friends, a lady, who is a member of the Association told me this:

> All during my childhood I saw colors in connection with people, but did not realize that it was uncommon. One day the appearance of a woman in our neighborhood struck me as odd, though I could not for the moment see anything strange about her. When I got home it suddenly struck me that she had no colors about her. Within a few weeks this woman died. That was my first experience with what I have learned to look upon as a natural action of nature.

Apparently the aura reflects the vibrations of the soul. When a person is marked for death the soul begins to withdraw and the aura naturally fades. At the end there is only a slim connection and the break is easy. I have heard that when people died suddenly, in accidents, the passing was very difficult because the way had not been prepared.

A person's aura tells a great deal about him, and when I understood that few people saw it and that it had a spiritual significance, I began to study the colors with an idea of discovering their meaning. Over a period of years I have built up a system which from time to time I have checked with other persons who see auras. It is interesting to note that in almost all interpretation these other people and I agree. We only differ with regard to the colors which are in our own auras. This is curious, for it shows how universal are nature's laws. We know that opposites attract and likes repel. Well, I have a lot of blue in my aura and my interpretation of this color does not always jibe with that of a person whose aura does not contain it and who therefore interprets it objectively. One lady I know has a great deal of green in her aura, and she is inclined to dislike green in the aura of others, and place a disagreeable interpretation on it, whereas it is the color of healing and a fine one to have.

Occasionally I have found in books devoted to occult sciences, definitions of colors, and these are generally in accord with what I have found by experience to be true. The reading of any particular aura, however, is a skill that is gained over a long period of time by constant observation and endless trial and error. The intermingling of the colors, their relationship one to another, and the dominance of one over the other, are matters which must be considered before rendering a judgment. I am generally better able to "read" persons I know than strangers, although certain general characteristics of the strangers, strike me immediately. But to be helpful I find it best to know the individual. Then I can tell him when I see the twinkling lights of success and achievement, or warn him when melancholy or illness threaten. Of course I do not do this professionally. I would not think of such a thing. But I believe it is an ability which all people will someday possess, and therefore I want to do what I can to get folks used to the idea of auras, so they will think in terms of auras, so they will begin to attempt to see themselves.

I have been told that with proper equipment it is possible for almost anyone to see an aura. Equipment has been built for this purpose, and I once met a professor who said that he not only had seen auras but in his laboratory had measured and weighed them.

Where do the colors come from, and what makes them shift and change? Well, color seems to be a characteristic of the vibration of matter, and our souls seem to reflect it in this three-dimensional world through atomic patterns. We are patterns, and we project colors, which are there for those who can see them.

In his remarkable book, *Pain, Sex, and Time*, Gerald Heard, speaking of the evidence for the evolution of consciousness, points out that our ability to see colors is expanding. The easiest color to see, as you know, is red. At that end of the spectrum the waves of light are long. At the other end, where blue runs into indigo and violet, the waves are short. According to Heard, who is a reliable scholar, our ability to see blue is very recent. Natives who live on the Blue Nile in Africa do not know it by that name. Their title for it, when translated, means brown. Homer, all through the Iliad and Odessey, describes the Mediterranean as the "wine-dark sea." Mr. Heard says that apparently Homer caught "the slight tinge of red in the purple of the Mediterranean," but did not see its predominant blue. Aristotle, moreover, said that the rainbow had only three colors: red, yellow and green. We all know that perspective in painting is recent, and it is apparently undeveloped in many primitive people to this day, for travelers in the remote Pacific Islands have found that natives looking at motion pictures are unable to perceive anything but a flat surface—their eyes cannot give three-dimensionality to the pictures.

So it would seem that our eyes gradually are gaining in power. I have heard many people comment on the prevalence of spectacles among our civilized people. They have seemed to consider this a bad thing. Could it be that it is a result of constant straining on the part of our eyes to see more and to bring us to the next step of evolution? I think this is true and will be recognized in the future. The Japanese, for instance, are just emerging from a medieval civilization, and in attempting to see the things we already perceive they have strained their eyes so that most every one of them wears glasses.

What will it mean to us if we make this next evolutionary step? Well, it will mean that we can see auras. What will this mean? I am going to answer that by telling two experiences of a friend of mine who is able to see auras.

This person, a woman, told me this:

> Whenever a person, whether it be a stranger, an intimate friend, or a member of my family, decides to tell me an untruth, or to evade a direct and frank answer to a question of mine, I see a streak of lemony green shoot through his aura, horizontally, just over his head. I call it gas-light green, and I have never known it to fail as an indication of evasion or falsification. I was a school teacher for many years, and my students marveled at my ability to catch them in any detour from the truth.

Imagine what that will mean—everyone able to see when you plan to tell them a lie, even a little white one. We will all have to be frank, for there will no longer be such a thing as deceit!

Now let me tell you the other incident.

> One day in a large city I entered a department store to do some shopping. I was on the sixth floor and rang for the elevator. While I was waiting for it I noticed some bright red sweaters, and thought I would like to look at them. However, I had signaled for the elevator, and when it came I stepped forward to enter it. It was almost filled with people, but suddenly I was repelled. The interior of the car, although well-lighted, seemed dark to me. Something was wrong. Before I could analyze my action I said, "Go ahead," to the operator, and stepped back. I went over to look at the sweaters, and then I realized what had made me uneasy. The people in the elevator had no auras. While I was examining the sweaters, which had attracted me by their bright red hues—the color of vigor and energy—the elevator cable snapped, the car fell to the basement, and all the occupants were killed.

You see what the knack of seeing auras will mean when it becomes a common ability. Danger, catastrophe, accidents, death, will not come unannounced. We will see them on their way as did the prophets of old; and as the prophets of old we will recognize and welcome our own death, understanding its true significance.

It is difficult to project ourselves into such a world, a world where people will see each other's faults and virtues, their weaknesses and strength, their sickness, their misfortunes, their coming success. We will see ourselves as others see us and we will be an entirely different type of person, for how many of our vices will persist when all of them are known to everyone?

One more comment on the possibilities of the future; then we will return to the more mundane present. Another person who sees auras once told me this:

> If I am talking to a person and he makes a statement of opinion which reflects a prejudice gained in one of his former lives, I see as he speaks a figure in his aura, which is a reflection of the personality he was in that time—I see, that is, the body of a Greek, or an Egyptian, or whatever he happened to be. As soon as we pass on to another subject and the opinion gained in that incarnation passes, the figure disappears. Later he will express another view. Perhaps he will say, "I have always loved Italy and wanted to go there," and as he speaks I will see the figure of a Renaissance man or an old Roman. During the course of an afternoon's conversation I may see six or eight of these figures.

Well, what is that but a Life Reading, except for the interpretations and judgments? It sounded so strange when I heard it that I was inclined to be skeptical, until one evening at dusk when, sitting on the porch of a friend's house, I saw the thing myself. My friend was speaking earnestly to a group of people, and he made some interpretation of English history. In his aura I saw the figure of a young monk, and I recalled that in his Life Reading this friend had been identified as a monk in England.

"But what do auras mean to the majority of people, who cannot see them," you ask? Well, the majority of people do see them, I believe, but do not realize it. I believe anyone can figure out what another person's aura is in a general way, if he will take note of the colors which a person habitually uses in the matter of clothing and decoration. How many times have you said of a woman, "Why does she wear that color? It does not suit her at all." How many times have you said, "How beautiful she looks in that dress. The color is just right for her. She was made to wear it." In both cases you have been reading an aura. The first woman was wearing a color which clashed with her aura. The second woman was wearing a color which harmonized with her aura. All of you know what colors are helpful to your friends, and bring out the best in them. They are the colors that beat with the same vibrations as the aura, and thus strengthen and heighten it. By watching closely you can even discover changes in your friends as they are reflected in a shift in the color predominating in their wardrobe.

Let me give you an example, one that has to do with health as it is indicated in the aura. I knew a man who from boyhood wore nothing but blue – frequently I have seen him with a blue suit, blue shirt, blue tie, and even blue socks. One day he went into a store to buy some ties. He was surprised to find that he had selected several which were maroon in color. He was even more surprised when as time went on, he began to choose shirts with garnet stripes and ties and pocket handkerchief sets in various shades of scarlet. This went on for several years, during which time he became more nervous and more tired. He was working too hard and eventually he had a nervous breakdown.

During this time the red had grown in prominence in his aura. Now gray, the color of illness, began to creep into the red, but as he recovered, the gray disappeared and then the blue began to eat up the red. Eventually all the red was consumed and he was well. Nor did he ever afterward wear anything red, scarlet, or maroon.

In another case a woman who ordinarily wore greens and yellows, went to a dress shop which she had patronized for years. The proprietress brought out several dresses but seemed perplexed when the lady tried them on. "I don't know what it is,'' the proprietress said, ''but you need something red or pink. I have never thought you could wear those colors but something in you seems to call for them now.'' The lady eventually bought a dress with red stripes. Within a month she was in a hospital, suffering from a nervous condition. She recovered, and continued to patronize the same dress shop, but the proprietress never again suggested that she wear red or pink.

Red

Red is the first of the primary colors and in ancient symbolism it represented the body, the earth, and hell, all three of which meant the same thing in the old mystery religions. The earth was the irrational world into which the soul descended from heaven. The body was the earth form which held the soul captive. Heaven was blue, and the spirit was blue. The mind was associated with yellow. It is interesting that in some systems of metaphysics blue is considered to be the true color of the sun; that is, if we could be outside earth we would see the sun as a blue light—soft, powerful, and spiritual. The yellow color is supposed to result from the collision of the sun's rays with the atmosphere of earth. Since the greatest spiritual weapon of man is his intellect, it is natural that mind be associated with the sun's color in this world.

As to the meaning of red, it indicates force, vigor and energy. Its interpretation depends upon the shade, and as with all colors, upon the relationship of other colors. Dark red indicates high temper, and it is a symbol of nervous turmoil. A person with dark red in his aura may not be weak outwardly, but he is suffering in some way, and it is reflected in his nervous system. Such a person is apt to be domineering and quick to act. If the shade of red is light it indicates a nervous, impulsive, very active person, one who is probably self-centered. Scarlet indicates an overdose of ego. Pink, or coral, is the color of immaturity. It is seen usually in young people, and if it shows up in the aura of one who is grown it indicates delayed adolescence, a childish concern with self. In all cases of red there is a tendency to nervous troubles, and such people ought to take time to be quiet and to get outside themselves.

Red is the color of the planet Mars, and corresponds to *do,* the first note in the musical scale. In early Christianity it signified the suffering and death of Christ, and was the color of war, strife and sacrifice.

Orange

Orange is the color of the sun. It is vital, and a good color generally, indicating thoughtfulness and consideration of others. Again, however, it is a matter of shade. Golden orange is vital and indicates self-control, whereas brownish orange shows a lack of ambition and a don't-care attitude. Such people may be repressed, but usually they are just lazy. People with orange in their auras are subject to kidney trouble.

In the early church orange signified glory, virtue, and the fruits of the earth, all of these being connected naturally with the sun. In the musical scale the note *re* corresponds to orange.

Yellow

Yellow is the second primary color. When it is golden yellow it indicates health and well-being. Such people take good care of themselves, don't worry, and learn easily; good mentality is natural in them. They are happy, friendly, and helpful. If the yellow is ruddy, they are timid. If they are red-heads they are apt to have an inferiority complex. They are thus apt often to be indecisive and weak in will, inclined to let others lead them.

In the musical scale the note *mi* corresponds to yellow, and Mercury is the planet of this color.

Green

Pure emerald green, particularly if it has a dash of blue, is the color of healing. It is helpful, strong, friendly. It is the color of doctors and nurses, who invariably have a lot of it in their auras. However, it is seldom a dominating color, usually being over-shadowed by one of its neighbors. As it tends toward blue it is more helpful and trustworthy. As it tends toward yellow it is weakened. A lemony green, with a lot of yellow, is deceitful. As a rule the deep, healing green is seen in small amounts, but it is good to have a little of it in your aura.

Saturn is the planet of this color, and *fa* is its musical note. In the early church it symbolized youthfulness and the fertility of nature, taking this quite naturally from the sight of the fields in spring.

Blue

Blue has always been the color of the spirit, the symbol of contemplation, prayer, and heaven. The sky is blue because gas molecules in the air cause light rays from the sun to be scattered. This is the scientific explanation but, as I have mentioned before, blue is said to be the true color of the sun, and it is also the color of the planet Jupiter, which is the ruler of great thoughts and high-mindedness.

Almost any kind of blue is good, but the deeper shades are the best. Pale blue indicates little depth, but a struggle toward maturity. The person may not be talented, but he tries. He will have many heartaches and many headaches, but he will keep going in the right direction. The middle blue, or aqua, belongs to a person who will work harder and get more done than the fellow with light blue, though there may be little difference between them in talent. Those with the deep blue have found their work and are immersed in it. They are apt to be moody and are almost always unusual persons, but they have a mission and they steadfastly go about fulfilling it. They are spiritual-minded for the most part, and their life is usually dedicated to an unselfish cause, such as science, art, or social service. I have seen many Sisters of Mercy with this dark blue, and many writers and singers also.

The musical note of blue is *sol,* and in the early church the color was assigned to the highest attainments of the soul.

Indigo and Violet

Indigo and violet indicate seekers of all types, people who are searching for a cause or a religious experience. As these people get settled in their careers and in their beliefs, however, these colors usually settle back into deep blue. It seems that once the purpose is set in the right direction, blue is a natural emanation of the soul. Those who have purple are inclined to be overbearing, for here there is an infiltration of pink. Heart trouble and stomach trouble are rather common to persons with indigo, violet and purple in their auras.

Venus is the planet of indigo, and *la* is its musical note. The moon is the planet of violet and *ti* is its musical note. In the early church indigo and violet meant humiliation and sorrow.

The perfect color, of course, is white, and this is what we all are striving for. If our souls were in perfect balance then all our color vibrations would blend and we would have an aura of pure white. Christ had this aura, and it is shown in many paintings of Him, particularly those which depict Him after the resurrection. You recall that He said at the tomb, "Touch me not for I am newly risen." He meant that as a warning, I think, for the vibrations of His being must at that time have been so powerful that anyone putting a hand on Him would have been killed—shocked as if by live wire.

Color is light, and light is the manifestation of creation. Without light there would be no life, and no existence. Light, in fact, is the primary witness of creation. All around us there are colors which we cannot see, just as there are sounds we cannot hear, and thoughts we cannot apprehend. Our world of comprehension is very small. We can only see the few colors between red and violet. Beyond red on one side and violet on the other are unguessed numbers of colors, some of them so bright and wonderful, no doubt, we would be stricken blind if by some chance we could see them.

But in the fact of these colors we cannot see, these sounds we cannot hear, these thoughts we cannot apprehend, lies the hope of evolution and the promise of eternity. This is a small and narrow world, and beyond it are the glories which await our souls. But if we labor to expand our understanding and our consciousness, we can push back the limits a little bit even while here, and thus see a little more, understand a little more.

Five hundred years before the birth of Christ, Pythagoras, the first philosopher, used colors for healing. Today medical science is just begining to see the possibilities in this method. If colors are vibrations of spiritual forces, they should be able to help in healing our deepest and most subtle maladies. Together with music, which is a kindred spiritual force, they form a great hope for therapy of the future.

But I do not think that color therapy will become widespread or practical until we have accepted the truth of auras and become accustomed to reading them in order to discover what imbalance is disturbing a person. Of course, we cannot transform all auras into a pure white light, but we can learn to detect signs of physical, mental and nervous disorders, and treat them in a proper way.

An aura is an effect, not a cause. Every atom, every molecule, every group of atoms and molecules however, simple or complex, however large or small, tells the story of itself, its pattern, its purpose, through the vibrations which emanate from it. Colors are the perceptions of these vibrations by the human eye. As the souls of individuals travel through the realms of being they shift and change their patterns as they use or abuse the opportunities presented to them. Thus at any time, in any world, a soul will give off through vibrations the story of itself and the condition in which it now exists. If another consciousness can apprehend those vibrations and understand them it will know the state of its fellow being, the plight he is in, or the progress he has made.

So, when I see an aura, I see the man as he is, though the details are missing. I believe the details are there, but they are missing from my perception and understanding. By experience I have learned to tell a good deal from the intensity of the colors, their distribution, and the positions they occupy. The aura emanates from the whole body, but usually it is most heavy and most easily seen around the shoulders and head, probably because of the many glandular and nervous centers located in those parts of the body. The dark shades generally denote more application, more will power, more spirit. The basic color changes as the person develops or retards, but the lighter shades and the pastels blend and shift more rapidly as the temperament expresses itself. The mind, builder of the soul, is the essential governing factor in the aura; but food, environment, and other conditions have their effect. Sometimes outside forces bring about a change. I once met a man in whose aura I saw a shaft of light, coming downward over his left shoulder. In it there was some white, a great deal of green, and a great deal of red with blue mixed in it. I read this as a sign that the man was receiving information inspirationally, which he was using for constructive purposes. I wondered if he was a writer, for it struck me that this would be a proper aura for such work. I asked him, and he told me that although he had been a writer, he was now engaged in lecturing and teaching, still giving information for the help of others.

The shape of the aura is sometimes helpful. In children, for instance, it is possible to tell whether a great deal of training by example will be needed, or whether precept will do as well. If the child is reasonable and will accept instruction on this basis the aura will be like a rolling crown. If example is needed, the aura will be a more definite figure, with sharp points and a variety of colors. If the child intends to be a law unto himself, the aura will be like a rolling chain, lower than the position of a crown, going about the shoulders as well as the head. In the green aura of healers, if the color quivers as it rises, the person is most sympathetic. Several times I have seen people in whose auras there were little hooks of light here and there. In each case the man had a job as overseer of large groups of other men, a director and a leader.

Let me give you a few examples of aura reading. These are not complete, just some notes that were taken one day at the end of our annual congress, when I was sitting with some of the members who had attended our meetings. Since I knew them all I gave them only an indication of the general condition of their auras.

A woman, middle-aged: Your aura has changed more in the last three days than any I have ever seen Your thoughts, your ideas, have wandered from the heights to the depths. At times the aura has been very beautiful, at others it has not been good. I have seen a great deal of the low, dull colors, about you. Evidently something has been worrying you. It is more mental than physical.

Young woman, a secretary: There has been a great deal of red about you lately, which means that you have been rather defiant. Often I have seen lines running away from your fingers when I can't see the aura about your face. That is probably because you think with your fingers, writing so much. In the last few days you have had a great deal of purple, which means the spiritual has mingled with your defiance; your desire and hope for better things has influenced your doubts and fears. You are sure, but a little fearful at times that you will not be able to put it over. You also have a great deal of coral and pink, meaning activity, but at times you smear it with more green than white, which indicates your desire to help others irrespective of themselves. That is not God's way.

Middle-aged woman, a teacher: There is a great deal of leaden gray in your aura, not only from your physical condition but because you have been doubting your own beliefs. You have become fearful of the thing to which you have entrusted your whole inner self. There also rise some smears of white, coming from your higher intellectual self, and from your spiritual intents and purposes. Broaden these. You also have a great deal of indigo, indicating spiritual seeking. There is green, but often fringed with red, for sometimes you would like to be in the other fellow's place, and would like him to be in your place, so that he'd know what you go through.

A middle-aged woman, social service worker: Your aura had been growing more and more to dark blue, golden, and white, with more and more white. I hope it won't entirely reach the halo, for then I would be fearful that you were leaving us. You have white with gold, which shows an ability to help others to help themselves. You have the ability to magnify the virtues of an individual, and minimize his faults.

Young woman, a clerk: Your aura is beautiful, yet often you become very fearful. At times you are easily dissatisfied. There is a great deal of blue, which is good. You should wear blue more often. You may not like it, but it will help you to think straight. You will be able to sing or hum more often as you work, if you wear blue. If you don't wear it outside, wear it close to your body. There are also some minerals to which you are susceptible, particularly green stones—not because of their healing quality for you, but because of the helpful influences they will enable you to give out to others. You control others a great deal by what you say and do, more so than you realize, yet there is a gret deal of coral in your aura, which means that you become fearful of your own choices and are unhappy in your environment.

Young woman, a nurse: In your aura there is a great deal of green, but you often rub it out with blue, then streak it up with red. I would not want to be around when you do the streaking, and most people who know you feel the same way, for when you let go it is quite a display of temper. You have a good deal of ability, especially in being able to act as a healing and helpful influence to others. Consequently, the principal color in your aura is green, but you streak it up when you desire to have your own way.

Young woman, a student: Your aura is changing. There is a great deal of indigo, indicating the seeker. This indigo is not always in a regular line, but looks more like tatting all around your head. I believe this indicates that there will be a change in your relationships with certain groups of people soon.

I have given these examples to show how colors blend to form an aura, and how they change from time to time. I do not expect that many of you will be able to see these colors around others, though I am sure some of you have the power without realizing it. You can become color-conscious, and you can learn to read auras from people's clothes and the colors you see predominant in their surroundings—their homes, their offices, even the colors of their automobiles, their dogs, and the flowers they have selected to grow in their gardens.

It can be a fascinating game, noticing how any person with vitality and vigor will have a little splash of red in a costume, in a room, or in a garden; noticing how persons who are quiet, dependable, sure of themselves, and spiritual, never are seen without deep blues—it is almost as if they turn things blue by being near them. Notice how bright and sunny people, who like to laugh and play, and who are never tired or downhearted, will wear golden yellow and seem to color things yellow, like a buttercup held under the chin.

Colors reflect the soul and the spirit, the mind and the body, but remember they indicate lack of perfection, incompleteness. If we were all we should be, pure white would emanate from us. Strive toward that, and when you see it in others, follow it as if it were a star. It is. But we who must take solace from smaller things can draw comfort from blue, get strength from red and be happy in the laughter and sunshine of golden yellow.

Color Chart

Color	Musical Note	Planet	Interpretation	Affliction
Red	Do	Mars	Force, Vigor, Energy	Nervousness, Egotism
Orange	Re	Sun	Thoughtfulness, Consideration	Laziness, Repression
Yellow	Mi	Mercury	Health, Well-being, Friendliness	Timidity, Weakness of Will
Green	Fa	Saturn	Healing, Helpful	Mixed with Yellow—Deceit
Blue	Sol	Jupiter	Spiritual, Artistic, Selfless	Struggle, Melancholy
Indigo	La	Venus	Seeking, Religious	Heart & Stomach Trouble
Violet	Ti	Moon	Seeking, Religious	Heart & Stomach Trouble

[illegible]

For more information or to receive a free catalog, call:

1-800-723-1112

[illegible]

Virginia Beach, VA 23451-0061

[illegible]

[illegible]